Second Edition

Strategic Reading 2

TEACHER'S MANUAL

T0346214

Kathleen O'Reilly
with Lynn Bonesteel

CAMBRIDGE
UNIVERSITY PRESS

32 Avenue of the Americas, New York NY 10013-2473, USA

Cambridge University Press is part of the University of Cambridge.

It furthers the University's mission by disseminating knowledge in the pursuit of education, learning and research at the highest international levels of excellence.

www.cambridge.org
Information on this title: www.cambridge.org/9780521281157

First published 2012

A catalogue record for this publication is available from the British Library

ISBN 978-0-521-28113-3 Student's Book
ISBN 978-0-521-28115-7 Teacher's Manual

ISBN 978-0-521-28115-7 Paperback

Layout services: Page Designs International, Inc.

Contents

Introduction

Strategic Reading is a three-level series for young adult and adult learners of English. As its title suggests, the series is designed to develop strategies for reading, vocabulary-building, and critical-thinking skills. Each level features texts from a variety of authentic sources, including newspapers, magazines, books, and Web sites. The series encourages students to examine important topics in their lives as they build essential reading skills.

The second level in the series, *Strategic Reading 2*, is aimed at high-intermediate level students. It contains 12 units divided into three readings on popular themes such as names, movies, dishonesty, and the senses. The readings in *Strategic Reading 2* range in length from 400 to 550 words and are accompanied by a full range of activities.

The units (and the readings within the units) can either be taught in the order they appear or out of sequence. The readings and tasks, however, increase in difficulty throughout the book.

There are 12 photocopiable unit quizzes on pages 37–48 of this Teacher's Manual, one for each unit of the Student's Book. Each one-page quiz contains a 150–175 word reading related to the unit theme and a half-page of tasks. The quizzes measure students' general reading comprehension, their ability to understand vocabulary in context, and their ability to use reading strategies. Suggested scores are included in the direction lines of the quiz tasks. An answer key for the quizzes is on pages 49–50 of this Teacher's Manual.

Student's Book Organization

The Unit Structure

Each unit has the same ten-page structure. It includes a one-page unit preview and three readings, each of which is accompanied by two pre-reading tasks and four post-reading tasks.

Unit Preview

Each unit begins with a brief summary of the three readings in the unit. These summaries are followed by questions that stimulate students' interest in the readings and allow them to share their knowledge of the topic.

Pre-Reading Tasks

Each reading is accompanied by two pre-reading tasks: a reading preview task and a skimming or scanning task.

Reading Preview

Before each reading, students complete one of four types of pre-reading exercises: *Predicting, Previewing Vocabulary, Thinking About the Topic,* or *Thinking About What You Know*. These exercises prepare students to read and help them connect the topic of the reading to their own lives. Students identify information they expect to read, learn new vocabulary, and write down what they know about the topic or mark statements that are true about themselves.

Skimming/Scanning

One *Skimming* or *Scanning* exercise accompanies every reading. Before reading the whole text, students learn either to scan a text to look for specific information or to skim a text to get the gist. Other activities in this section ask students to confirm predictions from the reading preview section, compare their experiences with the writer's experiences, or identify the writer's opinion.

Post-Reading Tasks

Following each reading are four post-reading tasks: A–D. These tasks respectively check students' comprehension, build their vocabulary, develop a reading strategy, and provide an opportunity for discussion.

A Comprehension Check

The task immediately following the reading is designed to check students' comprehension. In some cases, students check their understanding of the main ideas. In others, students have to delve more deeply into the text for more detailed information.

B Vocabulary Study

This section is designed to help students understand six to eight words that appear in the text. Students use contextual clues, recognize similarity in meaning between words, or categorize words according to meaning.

C Reading Strategy

An important part of *Strategic Reading* is reading strategy development. Students are introduced to a variety of strategies, such as making inferences, recognizing purpose, and paraphrasing. (For a full list of reading strategies, see the Scope and Sequence on pages iv–v.) Practicing these strategies will help students gain a deeper understanding of the content of the text and develop the necessary strategies they will need to employ when they read on their own outside of the classroom. The section opens with a brief explanation of the reading strategy and why it is important.

D Relating Reading to Personal Experience

This section asks three open-ended questions that are closely connected to the topic of the reading. It gives students an opportunity to share their thoughts, opinions, and experiences in discussion or in writing. It is also a chance to review and use vocabulary introduced in the text.

Timed Reading

Each unit ends with an invitation for students to complete a timed reading task. Students are instructed to reread one of the texts in the unit, presumably the one they understand best, and to time themselves as they read. They then record their time on page 121 and calculate their words per minute reading speed, which they enter in the chart on page 124. In this way, they can check their progress as they proceed through the book. (Naturally, there is no harm in students rereading and timing themselves on every text in a unit. However, this could be demotivating for all but the most ambitious of students.)

Reading Strategies

Reading is a process that involves interaction between a reader and a text. A successful reader is a strategic reader who adjusts his or her approach to a text by considering questions such as:

- What is my purpose in reading this text? Am I reading it for pleasure? Am I reading it to keep up-to-date on current events? Will I need this information later (on a test, for example)?

- What kind of text is this? Is it an advertisement, a poem, a news article, or some other kind of text?

- What is the writer's purpose? Is it to persuade, to entertain, or to inform the reader?

- What kind of information do I expect to find in the text?

- What do I already know about texts of this kind? How are they usually organized?

- How should I read this text? Should I read it to find specific information, or should I look for the main ideas? Should I read it again carefully to focus on the details?

- What linguistic difficulties does the text pose? How can I deal with unfamiliar vocabulary, complex sentences, and lengthy sentences and paragraphs?

- What is my opinion about the content of the text?

Reading strategies are the decisions readers make in response to questions like these. Reading strategies may prompt the reader to make predictions about the content and organization of a text based on background knowledge of the topic as well as familiarity with the text type. They may help the reader decide the rate at which to read the text – a quick skim for main ideas; a scan for specific information; a slower, closer reading for more detailed comprehension; or a rapid reading to build fluency. Other reading strategies help the reader make sense of the relationships among the ideas, such as cause and effect, contrast, and so on. In addition, the strategy of reading a text critically – reacting to it and formulating opinions about the content – is a crucial part of being a successful reader.

The *Strategic Reading* series develops fluency and confidence in reading by developing the student's repertoire of reading strategies. Students learn how to approach a text, how to choose appropriate strategies for reading a text, how to think critically about what they read, and how to deal with the difficulties that different kinds of texts may pose.

Jack C. Richards

Teaching Tips

The *Strategic Reading* series emphasizes reading rather than speaking or writing. However, every task should always involve some oral activity, since students should be encouraged to explain their answers in pairs, groups, or to the class. In addition, if your class is sufficiently advanced and if time permits, have students write their answers when appropriate. If students write their answers, find ways to have them discuss what they have written. For example, place students in pairs or groups to exchange and read each other's writing and then discuss it. Then have one member of the pair or group verbally summarize the discussion or tell the class one or two interesting ideas from the discussion.

Unit Preview Page

This page engages students' interest in the topic and gives them a visual and verbal preview of the three readings in the unit.

Although the instruction at the top of the page asks students to answer the questions for a reading just before they read it, you may prefer to have students respond to the questions for all three readings before they begin the unit.

Give students time to read the descriptions of the readings and the questions before initiating discussion. Make sure students understand the vocabulary on this page, and answer any questions they may have.

Pre-Reading Tasks

The first of these two tasks is either *Predicting*, *Previewing Vocabulary*, *Thinking About the Topic*, or *Thinking About What You Know*. The second task is either *Skimming* or *Scanning*. Make sure students understand that skimming is a quick reading for general ideas, whereas scanning is a quick reading to find specific information. Students usually do these tasks by themselves and then compare answers with a partner.

Take your time with these tasks. The more secure students feel with their grasp of the topic and the vocabulary, the better their reading experience will be.

Comprehension Check (Post-Reading Task A)

In this section, students do tasks such as answering questions about the reading, correcting mistakes in a paragraph about the reading, deciding whether statements about the reading are true, and identifying which paragraphs discuss particular ideas.

Encourage students to go back to the text to find or check their answers, and then discuss in pairs or small groups how they arrived at their answers.

Vocabulary Study (Post-Reading Task B)

In this study of six to eight words from the reading, students use contextual clues to identify meaning, recognize similarity in meaning between words, or categorize words according to meaning.

Note that the definitions or meanings given in these vocabulary tasks are specifically relevant to the readings. That is, the word may have other meanings in other contexts. If time permits and if the students are interested, don't hesitate to discuss other possible meanings when appropriate.

The vocabulary in these tasks was chosen because it is critical for students' understanding of the text at hand and useful for further reading, as well. In addition to single words, idioms and phrases are sometimes included in this section. You always have the option of teaching more vocabulary, however. In this Teacher's Manual, a few suggestions for additional vocabulary are provided after the answers to the Vocabulary Study tasks.

Reading Strategy (Post-Reading Task C)

The Scope and Sequence, on pages iv–v of the Student's Book, shows which strategies are taught in each unit. The list below is an alphabetized list of all the reading strategies in *Strategic Reading 2* with some additional information about the strategy and how to teach it. The reading strategies in Post-Reading Task C all involve critical-thinking skills.

Identifying Main Ideas and Supporting Details: Understanding the difference between main ideas and supporting details is often difficult for students. Therefore, there are several types of tasks in *Strategic Reading* that practice this strategy. For example, sometimes students are asked to distinguish between a main idea and a supporting detail. Other times, students have to find examples (details) in the text to support general statements. Remind students that the main idea of a paragraph is often – but not always – in the first or last sentence. The main idea of the whole reading is often – but not always – in the first or last paragraph.

Making Inferences: As students work through the inference questions, have them identify the place(s) in the text that led them to make the inferences. This will help students see that an inference is not a blind guess but rather a logical conclusion based on information in the text.

Organizing Information into a Chart: In this type of task, students complete a chart to deepen their understanding of the text by seeing the information in a new way. Point out to students that in the future they can adopt this strategy by making their own charts to help them understand a particular text or study for a test.

Paraphrasing: Paraphrasing is also difficult for students because they tend to want to simply repeat the original text. Have them practice by paraphrasing some information that you tell them verbally and that has nothing to do with the text at hand. You could also demonstrate by paraphrasing some things that the students tell you. Explain that paraphrasing practice is not only good for cementing their understanding of an idea but is also a good opportunity for them to practice their vocabulary.

Recognizing Cause and Effect: In one task, students are asked to determine if statements from the reading are either causes or effects. In another task, students are presented with two lists – one of causes and the other of effects – and asked to match the right cause with the right effect. When students first encounter these cause and effect tasks, you might want to help them by doing the first two or three items together as a class.

Recognizing Contrast in a Text: Being able to identify words that signal contrast is as important as understanding the ideas or events being contrasted. Students practice recognizing the signal words in this task. You might also ask them to keep a list of words that signal contrast in their notebooks or in an electronic file, adding to the list as they discover more of these words in their reading.

Recognizing Point of View: Explain to students that sometimes writers present their own points of view and sometimes they present the points of view of others. Also remind students that sometimes the writer does not express a point of view at all.

Recognizing Purpose: Before students do the first task of this type, elicit reasons why someone might write a work of nonfiction. Does the writer want to give general information about a topic? Is the writer's purpose to give specific information about one aspect of a topic? Does the writer want to persuade or convince the reader in some way? What are some other reasons? After students have had a chance to think about and discuss this question, have them do the task.

Summarizing: Students usually have trouble summarizing what they have read. They often want to include unnecessary details. One way to help them is to elicit the main idea(s) of the reading before they begin the summarizing task. If your class is sufficiently advanced, ask them to write one-paragraph summaries of any of the readings. However, be aware of another pitfall of written summaries: students sometimes copy directly from the text. Make sure they understand that complete sentences or longer passages taken directly from the text must have quotation marks and that quotations in brief summaries should only be used sparingly.

Thinking Beyond the Text: This task gives students the opportunity to decide where passages of additional material on the topic could fit into the text. Be sure that students clearly explain the reasons for their answers.

Understanding Pronoun Reference: Students often misunderstand a text if they have trouble identifying the words that the pronouns refer to. Where appropriate, point out to students that the pronouns *it*, *they*, and *them*, as well as the determiners *this*, *that*, *these*, and *those*, can refer not only to nouns but also to entire ideas.

Understanding Reference Words and Phrases: This task is similar to that of understanding pronoun reference. It will help students understand that pronouns are not the only way to indicate reference in a text.

Understanding Text Organization: In this task, students are asked to read a list of topics and then number each topic according to the order in which it appears in the text. The listed topics are purposely out-of-order so that students must analyze the text organization for the purpose of numbering them correctly. If appropriate for your class, make students aware that carefully considering the order of topics in a text is also a strategy they can use to check the logic of their own writing.

Understanding the Order of Events: This strategy differs from the one above in that it concerns specific events rather than topics. In this task, students number a list of steps from first to last to clarify the order in which the events happened.

Visualizing Information in a Text: This type of task presents photographs or drawings of events described in the text. Students must identify the events illustrated, which reinforces their understanding of the reading. Encourage students to adopt this strategy by making rough drawings (or detailed ones if they are artistically inclined) of events in other texts where appropriate.

Relating Reading to Personal Experience (Post-Reading Task D)

The three open-ended questions in this task encourage students to share their thoughts and opinions related to the reading. Students can work in pairs or groups. Circulate among the students and guide them in using vocabulary from the readings when possible. If time permits, a member of each pair or group can share their ideas with the class. If your class is sufficiently advanced, you might have students write a paragraph or short essay in response to a question of their choice.

Timed Reading

Make clear to students that doing timed readings is not a test. Rather, each student's goal should be to improve his or her reading speed over time and with a lot of practice. There is no "correct" amount of time in which to complete a reading.

Read through the instructions on page 121 of the Student's Book with the students and answer any questions. You can suggest some helpful pointers, such as: *Read the text straight through, without going back to reread any parts. Don't stop to look up any words. When you see words that you don't know or remember, just skip over them. Slow down a little when you get to important parts, such as main ideas, to make sure you understand them.*

1 Names

Unit Preview Page 1

This page engages students' interest in the topic of names and gives them a visual and verbal preview of the three readings in Unit 1: "What's Your Name?," "Do People Like Their Names?," and "The Right Name."

Pre-teach any vocabulary on this page that you think students might have difficulty understanding.

Suggested Additional Vocabulary

form (par. 1): a document, either paper or electronic, that has spaces where you fill in information

single (par. 2): not married

truly (par. 7): in this context, it means *really*; it can also mean *sincerely* – for example, *I am truly sorry* – or in *Yours truly*, as an alternative to *Sincerely (yours)* at the end of a letter.

Reading 1

What's Your Name? Page 2

This article shows how cultural differences in names can cause problems for people when they fill out electronic forms for databases.

Predicting Page 2

Answers will vary.

Skimming Page 2

Answers
3, 4

A Comprehension Check Page 3

Answers
1. c
2. d
3. d

B Vocabulary Study Page 4

Answers
1. siblings
2. precedes
3. fill out
4. enter
5. accommodate
6. indicates

C Recognizing Point of View Page 4

Answer
4

D Relating Reading to Personal Experience Page 4

Answers will vary.

Reading 2

Do People Like Their Names?
Page 5

This newspaper article is about peoples' different feelings about their first names.

Thinking About the Topic Page 5

Answers will vary.

Skimming Page 5

> **Answers**
> 1. D
> 2. E
> 3. D
> 4. E
> 5. D (Some students may think people mispronounce Ember's name, too, because often she is called "Amber." This is not a mispronunciation; more likely, they've never heard the name "Ember" and call her by the name they probably know: Amber. If students mention this, however, you might praise them for noticing.)

A Comprehension Check Page 6

> **Answers**
> a. 3   c. 1
> b. 4   d. 2

B Vocabulary Study Page 7

> **Answers**
> 1. f   5. g
> 2. d   6. a
> 3. c   7. e
> 4. b

> **Suggested Additional Vocabulary**
>
> **ember** (photograph and par. 4): when not used as a proper name, it means a small piece of wood or coal that continues to burn without a flame as a fire dies down
>
> **shy** (par. 1): uncomfortable with other people and unwilling to talk to them
>
> **make fun of** (par. 1): make a joke about

C Making Inferences Page 7

> **Answers**
> 1, 2, 3, 5, 6

D Relating Reading to Personal Experience Page 7

Answers will vary.

Reading 3

The Right Name Page 8

The importance of choosing the right name for a company – and how five successful companies did it – is discussed in this reading.

Thinking About the Topic Page 8

Answers will vary.

Scanning Page 8

> **Answers**
>
> | Company Names | Original Names |
> | --- | --- |
> | Google | BackRub |
> | Nike | Blue Ribbon Sports |
> | PepsiCo | Pepsi-Cola |
> | Yahoo | Jerry and David's Guide to the World Wide Web |
> | Xerox Corporation | Haloid Company |

You might point out to students that in this task, the word "original" has a different meaning from its use in paragraph 4 of "Do People Like Their Names?" on page 6 of the Student's Book. In that reading, Ember uses "original" to mean *unique*.

A Comprehension Check Page 9

> **Answers**
> 1. Xerox
> 2. Yahoo
> 3. PepsiCo
> 4. Xerox; Nike
> 5. Google

B Vocabulary Study Page 10

Answers

1. makes you think of
2. didn't spell
3. accidentally
4. make it available
5. a similar or the same
6. bubbles

Suggested Additional Vocabulary

search engine (par. 2): a computer program used for finding specific information on the Internet

catchy (par. 4): appealing and easy to remember

technique (par. 5): a special way or method of doing something

Optional Unit Activity

Put students in groups and ask each group to choose one of the following projects:

1. Design the name portion of a personal information form that is suitable for the names of everyone in the class.

2. Imagine that you are designing a search engine to compete with Google and Yahoo. Decide on what you would call it – and why.

Have each group share its work with the class.

C Organizing Information into a Chart
Page 10

Answers

Name of company	Person(s) who started company	Original name of company	Origin of current name of company
Google		BackRub	misspelling of *googol*
Yahoo	Jerry Yang and David Filo	Jerry and David's Guide to the World Wide Web	a catchy word in the dictionary
Xerox		Haloid	xerography
Nike	Phil Knight	Blue Ribbon Sports	the Greek goddess of victory
PepsiCo	Caleb Bradham	Pepsi-Cola	pepsin and cola nuts

D Relating Reading to Personal Experience Page 10

Answers will vary.

2 Helping Others

Unit Preview Page 11

This page engages students' interest in the topic of helping other people and gives them a visual and verbal preview of the three readings in Unit 2: "Don't Just Stand There," "Random Acts of Kindness," and "Monkey Business."

Pre-teach any vocabulary on this page that you think students might have difficulty understanding.

Reading 1

Don't Just Stand There Page 12

This reading discusses typical ways that people react in emergency situations and suggests some reasons for their behavior.

> #### Cultural Note
>
> **911** is the number you dial in the United States to get help in emergencies. Calls to 911 are answered by an operator who is trained to ask you some questions in order to determine which emergency service you need – usually the fire department, the police, or a hospital. Note that 911 is for emergencies only.

Thinking About the Topic Page 12

Answers will vary.

Skimming Page 12

> #### Answer
> The writer includes all of the reasons.

A Comprehension Check Page 13

> #### Answers
> a. 7   e. 5
> b. 2   f. 1
> c. 6   g. 4
> d. 3

B Vocabulary Study Page 14

> #### Answers
> 1. deterrent
> 2. sensitive
> 3. ambiguous
> 4. cues
> 5. assistance
> 6. inclination

> #### Suggested Additional Vocabulary
>
> **competent** (par. 2): having the skills and ability to do something
>
> **rationalizing** (par. 7): creating a reason, explanation, or excuse for something
>
> **evaluate** (par. 7): analyze, judge

C Identifying Supporting Details
Page 14

> #### Answers
> 1. a. someone else may be able to help better
>   b. fear of embarrassment
>   c. maybe there is no problem - no one else looks concerned
> 2. a. the situation may be ambiguous – not really sure if there's a problem
>   b. the bystander effect – the more people observing an emergency, the less responsible each one of them personally feels

D Relating Reading to Personal Experience Page 14

Answers will vary.

Reading 2

Random Acts of Kindness Page 15

This article from the Internet shows some ways that we can make life a little more pleasant for other people.

Predicting Page 15

Answers will vary.

Skimming Page 15

Answer

1

A Comprehension Check Page 16

Answers

1. d	4. c
2. a	5. f
3. e	6. b

B Vocabulary Study Page 17

Answers

1. e	4. f
2. a	5. c
3. b	6. d

Suggested Additional Vocabulary

for days (par. 5): for many days, that is, for a long time

placemat (par. 5): a piece of cloth, paper, or plastic put on a table under a person's plate and eating utensils

graffiti (par. 8): writings or drawings made on surfaces in public places

C Visualizing Information in a Text
Page 17

Answers

1. plant flowers
2. paint classrooms
3. prepare hot meals for the hungry
4. put a coin into a stranger's parking meter
5. pay someone's bridge toll
6. put some money into a needy woman's hand

D Relating Reading to Personal Experience Page 17

Answers will vary.

Reading 3

Monkey Business Page 18

This article presents a real-life example of a monkey who is trained to help paralyzed people and how she helps her owner.

Predicting Page 18

Answers will vary.

Skimming Page 18

Answers

1, 2, 3, 6

A Comprehension Check Page 19

Answers

a. 4	e. 3
b. 5	f. 1
c. 7	g. 6
d. 2	

B Vocabulary Study Page 20

Answers

1. f	4. b
2. e	5. a
3. d	6. c

Suggested Additional Vocabulary

takes over (par. 3): replaces (someone)

laser (par. 4): a device that produces a powerful, highly controlled, narrow beam of light

never gains an ounce (par. 5): doesn't gain any weight

C Summarizing Page 20

Possible answers

1. help / assist
2. tasks
3. paralyzed / a quadriplegic
4. home
5. laser / light
6. family

D Relating Reading to Personal Experience Page 20

Answers will vary.

Optional Unit Activity

Give students some time to think about and list random acts of kindness or senseless acts of beauty that would be practical for them to perform in the next week.

Then ask them to keep a journal during the week noting which of those acts they actually did and people's reactions to the actions. They could also note in their journals whether or not during that week they observed anyone in an emergency situation, and if so, what happened.

At the end of the week, put students in groups to discuss their experiences. Have one member of each group share some of what the group discussed with the class.

3 Movies

Unit Preview Page 21

This page engages students' interest in the topic of the movies and gives them a visual and verbal preview of the three readings in Unit 3: "A Dangerous Career in the Movies," "Life as a Movie Extra," and "The Storyteller."

Pre-teach any vocabulary on this page that you think students might have difficulty understanding.

Reading 1

A Dangerous Career in the Movies Page 22

In this article, you will find out what a stunt person is and why movie companies use stunt people.

Predicting Page 22

Answers will vary.

Skimming Page 22

Answers

2, 3, 4

A Comprehension Check Page 23

Answer

3

B Vocabulary Study Page 24

Answers

1. replace
2. careful
3. a long time before
4. very careful
5. a general idea
6. made

Suggested Additional Vocabulary

(what) comes to mind? (par. 1): (what) do you think of?

thrill (par. 3): a feeling of great excitement and pleasure

rehearsed (par. 3): practiced

C Identifying Supporting Details

Page 24

Answers

1. Any two of the following:
   SD: par. 1: *This work is too dangerous for regular actors.*
   SD: par. 2: *If the actors injure themselves, it can delay the production schedule.*
   SD: par. 2: *Using stunt people also saves time.*
   SD: par. 2: *Most stunt people have years of experience, which enables them to perform their stunts with a minimum of risk.*
   SD: par. 2: *It would take too long to train the actors to perform dangerous scenes safely.*

2. Any two of the following:
   SD: par. 3: *careful planning*
   SD: par. 3: *attention to detail*
   SD: par. 3: *extreme caution*
   SD: par. 3: *have to know what to do if anything goes wrong*
   SD: par. 4: *being in top physical condition*

3. Any two of the following:
   SD: par. 4: *dangerous sports*
   SD: par. 4: *rescue work*
   SD: par. 4: *the military*
   SD: par. 4: *an area that involves strong physical conditioning and has an element of physical danger*
   SD: par. 4: *martial arts*
   SD: par. 4: *scuba diving*
   SD: par. 4: *wrestling*

4. Any two of the following:
   SD: par. 5: *stunts that would be too dangerous or expensive for real stunt people to perform*
   SD: par. 5: *big fight scenes*
   SD: par. 5: *car crashes*
   SD: par. 5: *explosions*

D Relating Reading to Personal Experience Page 24

Answers will vary.

Reading 2

Life as a Movie Extra Page 25

This article shows that being a movie extra has its rewards, but it isn't as glamorous as you may think.

Thinking About What You Know Page 25

Answers will vary.

Skimming Page 25

Answers
1. F
2. T
3. F
4. T
5. F
6. T

A Comprehension Check Page 26

Answers
These answers should be crossed out:
1. c
2. c
3. b
4. b

B Vocabulary Study Page 27

Answers
1. fellow
2. background
3. parts
4. behind the scenes
5. shoot
6. attracted to

C Thinking Beyond the Text Page 27

Answers
a. par. 3
b. par. 5
c. par. 1
d. par. 2
e. par. 4

D Relating Reading to Personal Experience Page 27

Answers will vary.

Reading 3

The Storyteller Page 28

This magazine article provides insight into the life of the popular moviemaker Steven Spielberg.

Cultural Note
The Boy Scouts of America (par. 3) is an organization for boys that encourages them to participate in outdoor activities and to become responsible and independent. The Girl Scouts is a similar organization for girls.

Predicting Page 28

Answers will vary.

Skimming Page 28

Answers
1. b
2. a
3. c

A Comprehension Check Page 29

Answers

a. 3   d. 1
b. 5   e. 2
c. 4

B Vocabulary Study Page 30

Answers

1. b   4. d
2. c   5. a
3. f   6. e

Suggested Additional Vocabulary

remains (par. 2): continues to be

He never looked back. (par. 4): *to never look back* is to never regret what you have done

passion (par. 5): an intense, powerful emotion

C Making Inferences Page 30

Answers

1, 6, 7

D Relating Reading to Personal Experience Page 30

Answers will vary.

Optional Unit Activity

Ask students to think of one of their favorite movies and make notes about how they would describe it to someone else. This could be done as homework. Encourage students to use vocabulary they have learned in this unit.

Then have each student describe his or her movie to the class without saying its title. The class should try to guess what movie it is.

4 Families

Unit Preview Page 31

This page engages students' interest in the topic of families and gives them a visual and verbal preview of the three readings in Unit 4: "Living with Mother," "Father's Day," and "The Sandwich Generation."

Pre-teach any vocabulary on this page that you think students might have difficulty understanding.

Reading 1

Living with Mother Page 32

A region of southwest China has an unusual approach to marriage, which is described in this article.

Cultural Note

The Mosuo people discussed in this reading are a Chinese ethnic minority who live in the Himalayas close to the Tibetan border. Their economy is largely based on agriculture.

There is quite a bit of interest in the Mosuo these days among anthropologists and cultural historians. Thus it is easy to find out more about them online simply by searching for "Mosuo."

Thinking About What You Know Page 32

Answers will vary.

Skimming Page 32

Answers
1, 3, 6, 7

A Comprehension Check Page 33

Answers
a. 7	e. 8
b. 3	f. 1
c. 2	g. 4
d. 5	h. 6

B Vocabulary Study Page 34

Answers
1. a	4. f
2. d	5. c
3. b	6. e

Suggested Additional Vocabulary
rarely (par. 2): almost never
closer to (par. 5): more connected emotionally
stable (par. 7): unlikely to change; secure

C Visualizing Information in a Text
Page 34

Answers
House A: 1, 4, 6, 9, 11, 13
House B: 2, 3
House C: 5, 12
House D: 7, 8
House E: 10, 14

D Relating Reading to Personal Experience Page 34

Answers will vary.

Reading 2

Father's Day Page 35

This excerpt from a memoir reveals a special and touching relationship a boy had with his aunt, who became his father figure after his father's death.

Previewing Vocabulary Page 35

Scanning Page 35

Answers

The author: stubborn, determined, softhearted, opinionated

Aunt Marion: compassionate, generous, opinionated, open-minded, stubborn, determined, softhearted

The author and Aunt Marion: stubborn, determined, softhearted, opinionated

A Comprehension Check Page 36

Answers

1. F – The writer's <u>father</u> died when he was very young.
2. F – The writer lived in Louisville, Kentucky, <u>after</u> his father's death.
3. F – The writer grew up with his mother, aunt, and <u>grandmother</u>.
4. T
5. F – Aunt Marion <u>wanted</u> to get married and have children.
6. T
7. F – The writer and his aunt <u>didn't agree</u> about everything.
8. F – For many years, the author has sent his aunt a <u>card</u> on Father's Day.

B Vocabulary Study Page 37

Answers

1. in your home
2. made the person decide to do it
3. don't get paid
4. are similar
5. it will certainly happen
6. praise

C Making Inferences Page 37

Answers

1, 4, 5, 6

D Relating Reading to Personal Experience Page 37

Answers will vary.

Reading 3

The Sandwich Generation Page 38

This article explains why many middle-aged people have become part of the "sandwich generation" in developed countries today.

Thinking About the Topic Page 38

Answers will vary.

Skimming Page 38

Answer

4

A Comprehension Check Page 39

Answers

1. b	3. a
2. b	4. b

B Vocabulary Study Page 40

Answers

1. D   5. D
2. S   6. D
3. S   7. D
4. D

Suggested Additional Vocabulary

ongoing (par. 1): continuing; not stopping

pressures (par. 1): difficult necessities

life expectancy (par. 2): the number of years a person will probably live

---

C Identifying Supporting Details
Page 40

Answers

1. SD: par. 1: *to look after their aging parents*

   SD: par. 1: *to help their young adult children deal with the pressures of life*

2. SD: par. 2: *. . . people are living longer than they used to.*

   SD: par. 2: *. . . these days young adults often live with their parents for a longer time than they did in the past.*

3. Any two of the following:

   SD: par. 3: *They may have to cover expenses that their parents cannot.*

   SD: par. 3: *They may have to manage their parents' financial and legal affairs.*

   SD: par. 3: *They may have to prepare for their parents' future needs, such as special medical care or a move to a nursing home.*

D Relating Reading to Personal Experience Page 40

Answers will vary.

Optional Unit Activity

Ask students to choose one member of their family who is or has been very significant to them. Here are some ideas for whom such a person might be:

- someone they were very close to as a child
- someone who helped them in a difficult situation
- someone who gave them particularly good advice about something
- someone whose character they admire
- someone who accomplished something extraordinary
- a deceased relative they have heard impressive stories about

As homework, have each student prepare a short presentation about the person he or she has chosen, including pictures if possible. Before students begin to prepare, review vocabulary from the unit that they might use in their presentations.

---

5 Men and Women

Unit Preview Page 41

This page engages students' interest in the topic of gender differences and gives them a visual and verbal preview of the three readings in Unit 5: "The Knight in Shining Armor," Men, Women, and TV Sports," and "Boys and Girls in Class."

Pre-teach any vocabulary on this page that you think students might have difficulty understanding.

Reading 1

The Knight in Shining Armor
Page 42

Relationships between men and women are explored in this fairy tale through traditional fairy-tale characters: a knight, a princess, and some dragons.

Predicting Page 42

Answers will vary.

Skimming Page 42

Answers
1. b   3. b
2. c

A Comprehension Check Page 43

Answers
a. 7   e. 3
b. 1   f. 4
c. 6   g. 5
d. 2

B Vocabulary Study Page 44

Answers
1. approved and accepted
2. kill
3. is loved by
4. moving her hands or head
5. happy
6. loudly
7. in danger

Suggested Additional Vocabulary

ashamed (par. 9): guilty and embarrassed about something you did or should have done

annoyed (par. 10): upset and irritated by someone or something

charged (par. 12): attacked quickly

C Making Inferences Page 44

Possible answers
1. She thinks her idea is better.
2. He didn't kill the dragon with his sword. He used the noose because the princess told him to use it.
3. He feels that now he is making his own decisions.
4. She is always telling him what to do, and he doesn't like it.

D Relating Reading to Personal Experience Page 44

Answers will vary.

Reading 2

Men, Women, and TV Sports
Page 45

This magazine article discusses differences in the ways men and women react to sports programs on TV.

Thinking About the Topic Page 45

Answers will vary.

Skimming Page 45

> **Answers**
> 1, 2, 4, 5, 6

A Comprehension Check Page 46

> **Answers**
> 1. Men: 51%; Women: 24%
> 2. Men 54%; Women: 34%
> 3. Men: over 50%; Women: 18%

B Vocabulary Study Page 47

> **Answers**
> 1. segment
> 2. let off steam
> 3. viewing
> 4. intake
> 5. prompts
> 6. rabid

> **Suggested Additional Vocabulary**
>
> **snacks** (par. 1e): light meals, or food eaten between meals
>
> **defeat** (par. 2): the loss of a contest; failure
>
> **counterparts** (par. 3): people having the same function or characteristics as another group – in this case, sports fans

C Recognizing Contrast in a Text
Page 47

> **Answers**
> 1. . . . [men also watch action-adventure and suspense programs]. [Women, (however,) would rather watch dramas, situation comedies, and soap operas.]
> 2. [Men watch sports to relax, follow a favorite team, see athletic drama . . . and have something to talk about.] [Women,) (on the other hand,) are more likely to watch for companionship.]
> 3. [A winning team puts men in a good mood] and prompts them to want to celebrate the victory. (But) [a losing team sometimes puts men in a bad mood] and they avoid their families for a while . . . .
> 4. He suggests that (while) [men tend to focus more on the moment of victory and defeat,] [women show a deeper interest in the athlete and the sport.]

D Relating Reading to Personal Experience Page 47

Answers will vary.

Reading 3

Boys and Girls in Class Page 48

This article discusses the differences in the ways boys and girls react to learning in the classroom.

Predicting Page 48

Answers will vary.

Skimming Page 48

> **Answers**
> 1. girls
> 2. Boys
> 3. Girls
> 4. Boys
> 5. Girls, boys

A Comprehension Check Page 49

Answer

2

B Vocabulary Study Page 50

Answers

1. reality check
2. wider implications
3. brilliant
4. motivation
5. restless
6. essential

Suggested Additional Vocabulary

report card (par. 6): a written document that evaluates how well or poorly a student is doing either through written comments, letter or numerical grades, or both

standards (par. 6): something established as a model or ideal; a level of achievement to aim for

estimations (par. 6): judgments or opinions about the value of something

C Recognizing Purpose Page 50

Answer

3

D Relating Reading to Personal Experience Page 50

Answers will vary.

Optional Unit Activity

Think of a fairy or folk tale from your culture that has to do with men and women, and tell the story to the class. Here are some possible themes (with examples from European traditions):

- a princess in danger who is saved by a handsome prince ("Sleeping Beauty")
- a beautiful young woman who is treated badly by others in her family ("Cinderella")
- an ugly creature who turns into a handsome prince ("The Frog Prince")
- a handsome man who saves a beautiful young woman from a witch's spell ("Snow White")

Many fairy tales from many cultures are easily found online.

Put the students into groups to discuss the meaning of the tale you told. Then have each group share their ideas with the class.

Alternatively – or additionally, if time permits – ask students to think of a tale about men and women from their cultures. Put them in groups to share their tales. Have each group decide on one tale to share with the class. Have the class discuss its meaning.

6 Communication

Unit Preview Page 51

This page engages students' interest in the topic of communication and gives them a visual and verbal preview of the three readings in Unit 6: "Spotting Communication Problems," "Watch Your Language!," and "What Is Text Messaging Doing to Us?"

Pre-teach any vocabulary on this page that you think students might have difficulty understanding.

Reading 1

Spotting Communication Problems Page 52

This article discusses how to improve your communication skills.

Thinking About What You Know Page 52

Answers will vary.

Skimming Page 52

Answers
1. d   3. b
2. a   4. c

A Comprehension Check Page 53

Answers
1. Do you make eye contact?
2. Do you talk with toys?
3. Do you avoid overspeak?
4. Do you interrupt?
5. [This picture should be circled.]

B Vocabulary Study Page 54

Answers
1. lag behind
2. composite
3. barriers
4. absorb
5. mannerisms
6. obscure

Suggested Additional Vocabulary
advance (par. 1): move ahead; be promoted
blocking (par. 2): stopping; preventing
make a mental note (par. 4): decide you will remember something

C Paraphrasing Page 54

Answers
1. a   3. a
2. a   4. b

D Relating Reading to Personal Experience Page 54

Answers will vary.

Reading 2

Watch Your Language! Page 55

This article explains how one family incorporates three languages into their lives.

Predicting Page 55

Answers will vary.

Skimming Page 55

1. He speaks to his wife in English.
2. He speaks to his children in English.
3. The children speak to their father in English.
4. The children speak to their mother in Catalan.

A Comprehension Check Page 56

1. F – In the writer's house, <u>three</u> languages are spoken.
2. T
3. F – The writer <u>does</u> understand / <u>understands</u> Catalan.
4. F – The writer <u>does</u> speak / <u>speaks</u> Spanish.
5. F – Julia is <u>not</u> upset because her parents don't speak to her in the same language.
6. T
7. F – Julia is <u>not</u> confused about which language to use with other children.
8. T

B Vocabulary Study Page 57

1. broken
2. keep up
3. assimilated
4. conclusion
5. restrict
6. relied on

Suggested Additional Vocabulary

thought back to (par. 9): remembered

mother tongue: (par. 12): native, or first, language

revealing (par. 14): showing or expressing something about someone or something, usually more than you might expect

---

C Understanding Reference Words and Phrases Page 57

1. the language that the writer's daughters speak
2. talk a lot
3. Sumpta and the writer
4. that my [the writer's] girls would grow up without speaking English
5. Spanish, English, Catalan

D Relating Reading to Personal Experience Page 57

Answers will vary.

Reading 3

What Is Text Messaging Doing to Us? Page 58

This reading discusses the pros and cons of text messaging.

Thinking About the Topic Page 58

Answers will vary.

Skimming Page 58

1, 2, 3, 4, 6

A Comprehension Check Page 59

a. 3	d. 1
b. 5	e. 2
c. 4	

B Vocabulary Study Page 60

Answers

1. g
2. d
3. f
4. a

5. c
6. b
7. e

Suggested Additional Vocabulary

convenient (par. 2): without difficulty; easy

the norm (par. 3): what is usually done; normal

influence (par. 4): the power to have an effect on something

C Recognizing Purpose Page 60

Answer

3

D Relating Reading to Personal Experience Page 60

Answers will vary.

Optional Unit Activity

Choose a few sentences from each reading that include Vocabulary Study words from those readings. You can simplify the sentences, but be sure to include the vocabulary words.

Create Textspeak versions of the sentences you chose, being especially careful to abbreviate the key vocabulary words.

Write your Textspeak sentences from the first reading on the board. Have students work in pairs to "decode" the sentences. Continue in the same way with your Textspeak sentences from the second reading and then the third reading.

Here are two examples of what you might write based on Reading 1, "Spotting Communication Problems":

- "Sumtms profs lag be'd in comm. skills."
  "Sometimes professionals lag behind in communication skills." (par. 1)
- "Spkng 2fast = 1 of the most c'm b'iers n comm'n."
  "Speaking too fast is one of the most common barriers in communication." (par. 5)

If you wish, allow students to look at the readings as they work on decoding your Textspeak.

7 Dishonesty

Unit Preview Page 61

This page engages students' interest in the topic of dishonesty and gives them a visual and verbal preview of the three readings in Unit 7: "The Telltale Signs of Lying," "Too Good to Be True," and "Truth or Consequences."

Pre-teach any vocabulary on this page that you think students might have difficulty understanding.

Reading 1

The Telltale Signs of Lying Page 62

This magazine article discusses why people lie and some clues that can help us determine if someone is lying or telling the truth.

Predicting Page 62

Possible answers
1. *Telltale signs* are signs that tell a story.
2. A person who is lying might not look directly at you / move around a lot / smile or laugh too much.
3. Her eyes are looking away, as though she wants to leave. She looks uncomfortable.
4. The main idea is probably that there are ways you can tell when people are lying.

Skimming Page 62

Answer
The main idea is that there are clues that tell us when people are lying.

A Comprehension Check Page 63

Answers
1. b   3. a
2. c

B Vocabulary Study Page 64

Answers
1. a   4. b
2. a   5. b
3. b   6. a

Suggested Additional Vocabulary
obvious (par. 2): clear; easy to see or understand
stay still (par. 4): not move; avoid moving
shifted (par. 5): changed

C Identifying Supporting Details
Page 64

Answers
1. verbal clues: they repeat the question; they give a vague answer

   nonverbal clues (*any two of the following*): they look as if they want to leave the room; they shift position; they cross their arms
2. behavior: they cover their mouths with their hands

D Relating Reading to Personal Experience Page 64

Answers will vary.

Reading 2

Too Good to Be True Page 65

This newspaper article explains that advertisements may not actually lie, but they often mislead.

Cultural Note
There is a well-known expression in English, "If it sounds too good to be true, it probably is."

Thinking About the Topic Page 65

Answers will vary.

Scanning Page 65

Answers

1. A company that makes paper towels might say that their product absorbs more water than other paper towels.
2. A makeup company might claim that their product does not rub off on your clothes.
3. Companies that make pain medications say that doctors prefer their products.
4. The purpose of the national advertising division of the Council of Better Business Bureau is to regulate advertising and to judge whether companies are telling the truth.

A Comprehension Check Page 66

Answers

1. F – Companies don't often have to prove their advertising claims. / Companies do often have to prove their advertising claims.
2. T
3. T
4. T
5. F – The advertising division of the Council of Better Business Bureau decided that the ColorStay ad was not completely false / was true.
6. T
7. T
8. F – Eighty-two percent of doctors did not prefer Orudis to other pain medications.

B Vocabulary Study Page 67

Answers

1. challenged
2. regulate
3. conducted
4. normal
5. impression
6. surveyed

Suggested Additional Vocabulary

decades (par. 3): a decade is a period of ten years

puzzled (par. 5): confused

prescription (par. 6): a doctor's written direction for the medicine that someone needs and how it is to be used

C Understanding Pronoun Reference
Page 67

Answers

1. a company
2. companies
3. the organization's advertising experts
4. another makeup company
5. the Council
6. that doctors preferred Orudis to all other pain medications

D Relating Reading to Personal Experience Page 67

Answers will vary.

Reading 3

Truth or Consequences Page 68

The writer of this newspaper article discusses the issue of cheating in schools.

Cultural Note

Truth or Consequences was the name of a popular quiz show on TV in the United States for several decades in the last half of the twentieth century. A contestant would be asked a trivia question. If the contestant couldn't answer the "truth" part correctly, he or she would be subjected to "consequences" – usually some silly or embarrassing stunt.

Thinking About What You Know Page 68

Answers will vary.

Skimming Page 68

Answers

1. more
2. many
3. More than
4. disagree
5. many

A Comprehension Check Page 69

Answers

a. 2	e. 8
b. 5	f. 7
c. 6	g. 1
d. 4	h. 3

B Vocabulary Study Page 70

Answers

1. e	4. a
2. d	5. b
3. f	6. c

Suggested Additional Vocabulary

ignoring (par. 4): pretending not to be aware of something

prohibit (par. 7): not allow; forbid

lifeguard (par. 7): a person at a swimming pool or beach whose job it is to make sure that people who swim are safe and to help them if they are in danger

C Visualizing Information in a Text
Page 70

Answers

a. 4	c. 2
b. 1	d. 3

D Relating Reading to Personal Experience Page 70

Answers will vary.

Optional Unit Activity

For homework, have students write (or make notes on) two stories about themselves: one that is true and one that is false.

Have the students tell each other their stories in small groups. After each story, have the group vote on whether it's true or false.

Discuss the experience as a class. How successful were they at detecting their classmates' lies? How did they decide whether someone was lying?

8 Etiquette

Unit Preview Page 71

This page engages students' interest in the topic of etiquette and gives them a visual and verbal preview of the three readings in Unit 8: "Cell Phone Yakkers Need Manners," "How Table Manners Became Polite," and "Dinner with My Parents."

Pre-teach any vocabulary on this page that you think students might have difficulty understanding.

Reading 1

Cell Phone Yakkers Need Manners Page 72

This newspaper article explores the dos and don'ts of cell phone etiquette.

Thinking About the Topic Page 72

Answers will vary.

Skimming Page 72

Answers
3, 4, 5

A Comprehension Check Page 73

Answers

1. d	4. b
2. a	5. c
3. e	

B Vocabulary Study Page 74

Answers
1. trouble
2. rude to
3. trying very hard to do
4. important
5. drive to the side of the road
6. remember

Suggested Additional Vocabulary

day care (par. 1): care provided for preschool-age children during the day by a professional caregiver so that the parents of the children can go to work

marital breakups (par. 5): divorces

deserve (par. 7): have the right to expect something either good or bad as a result of one's actions

C Recognizing Point of View Page 74

Answer
3

D Relating Reading to Personal Experience Page 74

Answers will vary.

Reading 2

How Table Manners Became Polite Page 75

This newspaper article discusses how table manners have evolved from thousands of years ago to today.

Thinking About What You Know Page 75

Answers will vary.

Skimming Page 75

Answers

All the table manners from the list should be circled. Answers about the individual table manners will vary.

A Comprehension Check Page 76

Answer

3

B Vocabulary Study Page 77

Answers

1. dipped
2. stale
3. wipe
4. fidget
5. picked out
6. greedy

Suggested Additional Vocabulary

grateful (par. 1): thankful

back then (par. 1): at that time; in the past

tidy (par. 6): neat; having everything in its correct place

C Making Inferences Page 77

Answers

1, 3, 5, 6

D Relating Reading to Personal Experience Page 77

Answers will vary.

Reading 3

Dinner with My Parents Page 78

This excerpt from Amy Tan's novel *The Joy Luck Club* describes a cross-cultural misunderstanding related to dining etiquette.

Cultural Note

In 1993, Tan's novel was made into a popular movie. The picture on page 78 is of a scene in the movie.

Predicting Page 78

Answers will vary.

Skimming Page 78

Answer

3

A Comprehension Check Page 79

Answers

1, 6, 8

B Vocabulary Study Page 80

Answers

1. slippery
2. chunk
3. coated
4. shrieking
5. burst
6. criticized
7. disparaging
8. proclaim

Suggested Additional Vocabulary

splayed (par. 2): spread wide apart

morsel (par. 3): a small piece or amount of food

platter (par. 8): large serving plate

C Paraphrasing Page 80

Answers

1. b   3. a
2. a

D Relating Reading to Personal Experience Page 80

Answers will vary.

Fear

Unit Preview Page 81

This page engages students' interest in the topic of fear and gives them a visual and verbal preview of the three readings in Unit 9: "Flying? No Fear," "Don't Fight a Good Fright," and "Stage Fright."

Pre-teach any vocabulary on this page that you think students might have difficulty understanding.

Reading 1

Flying? No Fear Page 82

This newspaper article discusses the common problem of the fear of flying – and one way to try to overcome it.

Thinking About the Topic Page 82

Answers will vary.

Skimming Page 82

Answer

All of the items are included in the reading.

A Comprehension Check Page 83

Answers
1. All
2. One
3. Some
4. None
5. Some
6. Some

B Vocabulary Study Page 84

Answers
1. land
2. obsessively
3. anxiety
4. trigger
5. patch
6. phobias

Suggested Additional Vocabulary

addressed (par. 3): discussed; dealt with

habit (par. 4): a particular act or way of acting that a person tends to do regularly

tension (par. 8): anxiety and worry

C Recognizing Cause and Effect
Page 84

Answers
1. C
2. E
3. E
4. C
5. C
6. E

D Relating Reading to Personal Experience Page 84

Answers will vary.

Reading 2

Don't Fight a Good Fright Page 85

The writer of this article offers some insights into why we enjoy being frightened.

Predicting Page 85

Answers will vary.

Skimming Page 85

Answer

3

A Comprehension Check Page 86

Answers

a. 2   d. 1

b. 5   e. 4

c. 6   f. 3

B Vocabulary Study Page 87

Answers

1. strange
2. an expert
3. imagine
4. satisfied
5. die
6. impossible
7. on purpose

Suggested Additional Vocabulary

manage (par. 2): control

resembles (par. 3): is similar to; seems like; looks like

expectations (par. 4): feelings or beliefs that something will or should happen

---

C Making Inferences Page 87

Answers

2, 3, 4, 6

D Relating Reading to Personal Experience Page 87

Answers will vary.

Reading 3

Stage Fright Page 88

This article explains that stage fright is common, even among professional performers, and it describes how some of them try to deal with it.

Previewing Vocabulary Page 88

Answers will vary.

Scanning Page 88

Possible answer

All the words relate to the nervousness / fears / stage fright of performers.

A Comprehension Check Page 89

Answers

1. F – Falling down onstage was ~~not~~ a good way for the pianist Vladimir Feltsman to deal with his stage fright.
2. T
3. F – Teachers and psychologists <u>can</u> help people with extreme stage fright.
4. T
5. T
6. T
7. F – Famous musicians ~~never~~ suffer from stage fright. / Famous musicians <u>sometimes</u> suffer from stage fright.
8. F – Famous musicians do ~~not~~ have to worry about performing well. / Famous musicians do ~~not have to~~ worry about performing well.

B Vocabulary Study Page 90

Answers

1. symptoms
2. mentors
3. fallible
4. tripped
5. wide-ranging
6. Visualizing

(know / learn something) inside out (par. 3): If you know something inside out, you know it extremely well. A similar idiom is to know something so well that you "could do / play it in your sleep."

at the root of (par. 5): the main reason for

principal (par. 6): main; head; chief

C Understanding Text Organization

Page 90

Answers

a. 5	d. 3
b. 1	e. 4
c. 2	f. 6

D Relating Reading to Personal Experience Page 90

Answers will vary.

Optional Unit Activity

Have students think of the scariest experience they have ever had in "real life," that is, not in a controlled situation such as an amusement park or while watching a movie. Examples might be a time they got lost or a time they were left home alone as a child. What was the experience? How did they survive it? With hindsight, could they have avoided the experience? Is there anything they would have done differently?

Then put students into groups to share their experiences. Encourage them to ask each other questions.

10 The Paranormal

Unit Preview Page 91

This page engages students' interest in the topic of the paranormal and gives them a visual and verbal preview of the three readings in Unit 10: "Psychic Solves Crimes," "A Near-Death Experience (NDE)," and "Mind over Matter."

Pre-teach any vocabulary on this page that you think students might have difficulty understanding.

Reading 1

Psychic Solves Crimes Page 92

This newspaper article reveals how a woman with psychic powers has helped London police solve crimes.

Previewing Vocabulary Page 92

Answers will vary.

Scanning Page 92

Possible answer

All the words relate to the topic of a psychic who helps the police solve crimes / catch criminals.

A Comprehension Check Page 93

Answers

1. Ms. Jones came to help us after the theft of *The Guitar Player*, painted by Johannes Vermeer. She began to have visions about the painting. She saw that it was in a cemetery in east London. We went to look for it and found it. The painting was in a newspaper.

2. There was a murder. Someone had killed an old woman. We took Ms. Jones to the room where the murder took place. She had a vision of the letters EARL and a red Cortina. We found out that a man had recently sold a red car at a place called Earl Motors. The man was the murderer.

B Vocabulary Study Page 94

Answers

1. d	4. c
2. e	5. b
3. f	6. a

Suggested Additional Vocabulary

secretly (par. 1): without the public (or anyone who is not directly involved) knowing some information

keep an open mind (par. 5): wait until you know all the facts before making a judgment

leads (par. 5): suggestions about ways to help solve a crime

C Making Inferences Page 94

Answers

1, 3, 4, 5

D Relating Reading to Personal Experience Page 94

Answers will vary.

Reading 2

A Near-Death Experience (NDE)
Page 95

This article from the Internet discusses the amazing similarities of near-death experiences among people of different cultures and ages.

Thinking About the Topic Page 95

Answers will vary.

Skimming Page 95

1, 2, 3, 6

A Comprehension Check Page 96

Answers
1. F – <u>Some</u> people who come close to death will have a near-death experience.
2. T
3. F – The characteristics of a near-death experience <u>do not</u> vary according to a person's culture.
4. T
5. F – Two different people <u>cannot</u> have exactly the same near-death experiences.
6. T
7. T
8. F – Researchers <u>do not</u> know why some people have NDEs and others do not.

B Vocabulary Study Page 97

Answers
1. background
2. bliss
3. coined
4. perception
5. voluntary
6. brilliant

Suggested Additional Vocabulary

meditating (par. 1): practicing the calming or clearing of your mind

standards (par. 3): accepted ways of doing things

tunnel (par. 4, bullet 2): a long passage under or through the earth, especially one made for cars and other vehicles

C Recognizing Purpose Page 97

Answer
3

D Relating Reading to Personal Experience Page 97

Answers will vary.

Reading 3

Mind over Matter Page 98

This article gives some examples to support the claim that the mind can be more powerful than the body.

Thinking About What You Know Page 98

Answers will vary.

Skimming Page 98

Answers
1, 4

A Comprehension Check Page 99

Answers
1, 3, 5, 6

B Vocabulary Study Page 100

Answers
1. e   4. a
2. c   5. b
3. f   6. d

Optional Unit Activity

In this activity, students can decide for themselves whether or not a Psi wheel works.

Put students into groups and have each group make a Psi wheel according to the instructions in the diagram on page 99.

After each group has made and tested their Psi wheel, discuss the experience as a class.

C Recognizing Cause and Effect

Page 100

Answers

1. c
2. b
3. d
4. a

D Relating Reading to Personal Experience   Page 100

Answers will vary.

11 Languages

Unit Preview Page 101

This page engages students' interest in the topic of language and gives them a visual and verbal preview of the three readings in Unit 11: "The Day a Language Died," "Aping Language," and "The Bilingual Brain."

Pre-teach any vocabulary on this page that you think students might have difficulty understanding.

Reading 1

The Day a Language Died Page 102

This article tells the story of the death of Catawba, a Native American language, and what it means for the world when a language dies.

Thinking About the Topic Page 102

Answers will vary.

Scanning Page 102

> **Answers**
> 1. b   3. c
> 2. a

A Comprehension Check Page 103

> **Answers**
> 1. c   3. b
> 2. a   4. c

B Vocabulary Study Page 104

> **Answers**
> 1. by heart
> 2. back
> 3. destiny
> 4. species
> 5. spread
> 6. extinction

> **Suggested Additional Vocabulary**
>
> **damage** (par. 3): harm; destruction
>
> **industry** (par. 3): the companies and activities involved in the production of goods for sale
>
> **fate** (par. 4): something that happens to a person or thing, especially something final or negative

C Making Inferences Page 104

> **Answers**
> 1, 3, 6

D Relating Reading to Personal Experience Page 104

Answers will vary.

Reading 2

Aping Language Page 105

In this magazine article, the writer discusses the controversy among researchers about whether apes can understand and produce language.

Previewing Vocabulary Page 105

Answers will vary.

Scanning Page 105

> **Possible answer**
> The words all relate to the topic of the language ability of apes and different opinions about it.

A Comprehension Check Page 106

B Vocabulary Study Page 107

Suggested Additional Vocabulary

impressive (par. 2): worthy and deserving of praise and admiration

distinguished between (par. 2): separated; recognized the difference between

colleagues (par. 3): the members of a group who work together

C Paraphrasing Page 107

D Relating Reading to Personal Experience Page 107

Answers will vary.

Reading 3

The Bilingual Brain Page 108

This article discusses how different parts of the brain influence language learning in people of different ages.

Thinking About What You Know Page 108

Answers will vary.

Skimming Page 108

A Comprehension Check Page 109

B Vocabulary Study Page 109

C Understanding Pronoun Reference

Page 109

Answers

1. English
2. children and adults
3. bilingual people
4. people were placed inside the MRI scanner
5. Kim and Hirsch
6. people from both groups
7. both groups of people
8. the way mothers teach a baby to speak / different methods involving touch, sight, and sound

D Relating Reading to Personal Experience Page 109

Answers will vary.

Optional Unit Activity

Ask if any students know friends, family members, or other people who speak three or more languages. Have those students interview the multilingual person, including questions such as the following:

- When did you learn each language?
- What were the circumstances that led you to learn these languages?
- Did you have any difficulties in learning these languages?

It may be that some of your students speak three or more languages, in which case, they can "interview" themselves.

Have the students give a report about their interviews to the class.

12 The Senses

Unit Preview Page 111

This page engages students' interest in the topic of the senses and gives them a visual and verbal preview of the three readings in Unit 12: "Ice Cream Tester Has Sweet Job," "Primer on Smell," and "How Deafness Makes It Easier to Hear."

Pre-teach any vocabulary on this page that you think students might have difficulty understanding.

Reading 1

Ice Cream Tester Has Sweet Job
Page 112

This newspaper article explains why being an ice cream tester is not about eating as much ice cream as you want to.

Predicting Page 112

Answers will vary.

Skimming Page 112

Answers
1, 3, 4, 5

A Comprehension Check Page 113

Answers

Do ...	Don't ...
drink herbal tea	drink coffee
taste a small amount	eat a lot before tasting
use a gold spoon	eat onions, garlic, or spicy food
spit out the sample	swallow the ice cream

B Vocabulary Study Page 114

Answers
1. avoid
2. order
3. stomach
4. caffeine
5. creamy
6. brands

Suggested Additional Vocabulary

discipline (par. 2): self-control

aroma (par. 3): smell – usually used to refer to a strong, pleasant smell

dairy (par. 3 & 5): milk and products made from milk

C Understanding the Order of Events
Page 114

Answers
a. 2	d. 5
b. 4	e. 1
c. 6	f. 3

D Relating Reading to Personal Experience Page 114

Answers will vary.

Reading 2

Primer on Smell Page 115

This article from the Internet provides a good introduction to the understanding of how our sense of smell affects our lives.

Thinking About What You Know Page 115

Answers will vary.

Skimming Page 115

A Comprehension Check Page 116

Answers

a. 3	e. 1
b. 7	f. 5
c. 4	g. 2
d. 6	

B Vocabulary Study Page 117

Answers

1. c	5. h
2. f	6. a
3. g	7. e
4. d	8. b

Suggested Additional Vocabulary

collect (par. 1): get; gather together

based on (par. 1): as a result of; because of

acute (par. 6 heading): strong

C Organizing Information into a Chart
Page 117

Answers

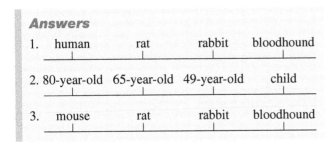

1. human   rat   rabbit   bloodhound

2. 80-year-old   65-year-old   49-year-old   child

3. mouse   rat   rabbit   bloodhound

D Relating Reading to Personal Experience Page 117

Answers will vary.

Reading 3

How Deafness Makes It Easier to Hear Page 118

This newspaper article explains some surprising facts about the relationship between deafness and the ability to hear music.

Predicting Page 118

Answers will vary.

Skimming Page 118

Answers

1. a	3. a
2. b	4. b

A Comprehension Check Page 119

Answers

1. F – According to Solomon, Beethoven's deafness made it easier to experiment when he was composing music.
2. T
3. F – Cochlear implants do not make it possible for deaf people to hear normally.
4. T
5. F – Cochlear implants do not help deaf people hear music.
6. F – A cochlear implant would not have helped Beethoven compose more easily.

B Vocabulary Study Page 120

Answers

1. obstacle
2. heightened
3. phenomenon
4. differentiate
5. rewarding
6. stimulus
7. clarity

C Summarizing Page 120

Answers

Deafness does not affect the ability of musicians to create music because they hear musical sounds in their head. ~~Maynard Solomon wrote about this in his biography of Beethoven.~~ Hearing devices like cochlear implants can help deaf musicians understand what people are saying, but the implants cannot help musicians hear musical sounds in the outside world. ~~In addition, it can take some time to get used to a cochlear implant.~~ Deaf musicians can only hear the musical sound inside themselves. ~~Therefore, a cochlear implant would not have helped Beethoven compose the Ninth Symphony.~~

D Relating Reading to Personal Experience Page 120

Answers will vary.

Optional Unit Activity

Tell each student to bring a strong-smelling item to the next class, for example: roses, chocolate, garlic, nail polish, soil, lemons. Ask them to put their items in some sort of container so that the odor cannot escape until the container is opened. (You may want to bring in an item or two of your own.)

Have all of the students except one close their eyes. Then ask that one student to open his or her container and walk around the room. See who can be the first to correctly identify the item based on its odor. Continue in this way until all of the students have had a chance to uncover their items.

Quiz • Unit 1

Read the text.

I started studying Spanish when I was in middle school. I was very *enthusiastic* 1
until our teacher started to *take attendance* on the first day of class. He *announced*
that he would give us each a Spanish name, which we would use during Spanish
class. He explained that this name would give us a new identity to *go with* the new
language we were learning.

At first, the idea didn't bother me. But as my classmates started to address me by 2
my new name, I began to feel uncomfortable. Why should I give up my identity in
order to learn a language? Using another name made me feel *ridiculous*.

I felt so silly using my Spanish name that I rarely spoke in class. As you can 3
imagine, I didn't *make* much *progress*. The next semester, we had a different
teacher, one who let us use our given names in class. As a result, I participated more
in class, and Spanish soon became my favorite subject.

Complete the exercises.

A Check (✓) the statement that best expresses the main idea of the reading. (*10 points*)

_____ 1. When the writer first started studying Spanish, she didn't like it very much.

_____ 2. The writer's name is important to her because it is related to her identity.

_____ 3. The writer's first Spanish teacher was not a very good teacher.

B Mark each statement *T* (true) or *F* (false). (*30 points*)

_____ 1. The writer wanted to learn Spanish.

_____ 2. The writer wanted to choose her own Spanish name.

_____ 3. At first, the writer wasn't upset about using a Spanish name.

_____ 4. The writer talked a lot in class.

_____ 5. The writer liked her second Spanish teacher better than her first one.

C Find the words and phrases in *italics* in the reading. Then circle the correct meanings.
(*60 points*)

1. When you are *enthusiastic*, you are **happy and energetic / worried and afraid**.

2. When you *take attendance*, you **call out names / invent new names**.

3. If you *announced* something, you **asked / told** people about a plan or decision.

4. If your shoes *go with* your clothes, they **look good / look bad** together.

5. If you feel *ridiculous*, you feel **embarrassed / excited**.

6. When you *make progress* in a subject, you **talk a lot / improve**.

Quiz • Unit 2

Read the text.

1   In some countries, the government has an important requirement for new doctors. After graduating from medical school, they must spend their first year working in very poor areas. These are typically places where health-care professionals are *reluctant* to work because of the difficult conditions. The doctors usually receive a stipend – or small salary – that is enough to cover their basic needs. In some cases, doctors are also given a free place to live.

2   This system is tremendously *beneficial*. First of all, it gives young doctors the opportunity to get valuable *hands-on* experience. Second, it provides poor people with a much-needed service. Most importantly, this type of program puts the needs of the public above the interests of individual doctors. It helps ensure that *prospective* doctors go into the field of medicine for the right reason – to assist others.

3   At a time when doctors' fees are very expensive, these *mandatory* community service programs remind doctors that their role as caregivers should always be the most important part of their work.

Complete the exercises.

A Find the words in *italics* in the reading. Then circle the correct meanings. (*50 points*)

1. If you are *reluctant* to do something, you **are sure** / **are not sure** that you want to do it.

2. If something is *beneficial*, it is **good** / **bad**.

3. With *hands-on* training, you learn something by **studying it** / **doing it yourself**.

4. A *prospective* teacher **has been a teacher for one year** / **wants to become a teacher**.

5. If something is *mandatory*, you **have to** / **want to** do it.

B Check (✓) the statement that best expresses the writer's point of view. (*10 points*)

_____ 1. Doctors should get more money for their community service work.

_____ 2. Doctors should not charge such high fees.

_____ 3. Doctors should understand that their most important role is to help people.

C Mark each statement *T* (true) or *F* (false). (*40 points*)

_____ 1. New doctors can always choose where they want to work.

_____ 2. In some countries, young doctors spend some time working with the poor.

_____ 3. Community service programs help rich people.

_____ 4. Doctors in community service programs get paid a lot of money.

Quiz • Unit 3

Name: _____

Date: _____

Read the text.

Today you can play a movie on your TV, computer, digital tablet, or smartphone   1
whenever and wherever you like. *Admittedly*, this is a wonderful *convenience*. But I
still prefer watching movies in a theater on a big screen.

One very simple reason is the *atmosphere* of the theater. Part of the enjoyment of   2
a movie is that it feels good to lose yourself in the world of the film. The darkened
theater, with its large screen and sound system, blocks out the real world. At home,
distractions from the real world can intrude on your movie-viewing pleasure.
Another reason is the social aspect of the theater. Even though my fellow viewers
and I don't talk during the movie, I still feel that we are sharing the experience. In
contrast, watching a film at home can make you feel *isolated*. Finally, many popular
films feature vivid special effects, amazing stunts, and scenes with *expansive* views.
The excitement of these scenes does not translate well onto small screens.

Complete the exercises.

A Check (✓) the four statements that you think the writer would agree with. (*40 points*)

_____ 1. Watching a movie at home is easier than going to a theater.

_____ 2. Watching a movie is a good way to forget the problems of everyday life.

_____ 3. You should spend a lot of money on a home theater with a big TV screen.

_____ 4. People should talk to each other when they watch a movie.

_____ 5. Watching a movie alone is less fun than watching it with someone else.

_____ 6. An action movie is more exciting when you watch it in a theater.

B Find the words in *italics* in the reading. Then match the words with their meanings.
(*60 points*)

_____ 1. *admittedly* (par. 1)   a. the feeling or mood of a place

_____ 2. *convenience* (par. 1)   b. interruptions

_____ 3. *atmosphere* (par. 2)   c. wide in area

_____ 4. *distractions* (par. 2)   d. something that makes life easier

_____ 5. *isolated* (par. 2)   e. alone; lonely

_____ 6. *expansive* (par. 2)   f. it is true that

Quiz • Unit 4

Name: _____

Date: _____

Read the text.

1   When I was growing up, my family always ate dinner together. It was the only time when we could all sit down to share a meal and talk about the events of the day. My friends *knew better than to* call during the dinner hour. The minutes between 5:00 p.m. and 6:00 p.m. were considered *sacred*.

2   These days, families in the United States rarely sit down to have dinner together. In homes where parents work and children play sports or do other *extracurricular* activities, everyone has a different schedule. In many households, the phones never stop ringing, and there is not even a specific dinnertime. Everyone just grabs something to eat whenever they get hungry. Family members are often so busy with their own interests that there is no time left to spend as a family.

3   Raising children and *instilling* a strong sense of family is not easy in today's *hectic* world. I still think, however, that parents should do whatever is necessary to make dinnertime the *invaluable* occasion that it once was.

Complete the exercises.

A Mark each statement *T* (today) or *P* (the past). *(40 points)*

_____ 1. The telephone is always ringing.

_____ 2. Families eat dinner together at the same time each day.

_____ 3. It's difficult to encourage children to appreciate family life.

_____ 4. Each family member has a busy schedule.

B Find the words in *italics* in the reading. Then circle the letters of the correct meanings. *(60 points)*

1. *knew better than to* (par. 1)
   a. knew they wouldn't
   b. knew they shouldn't
   c. knew they had to

2. *sacred* (par. 1)
   a. very interesting
   b. very important
   c. very difficult

3. *extracurricular* (par. 2)
   a. not part of regular school
   b. part of regular school
   c. extra homework

4. *instilling* (par. 3)
   a. destroying
   b. creating
   c. preventing

5. *hectic* (par. 3)
   a. very dangerous
   b. very unhealthy
   c. very busy

6. *invaluable* (par. 3)
   a. very useful
   b. very exciting
   c. very expensive

Quiz • Unit 5

Name: _____

Date: _____

Read the text.

Although most people form *numerous* friendships during their lives, the kinds of   1
friendships that women develop are unlike those of men.

The differences probably begin in childhood. Little girls usually spend most   2
of their time with one "best friend." Little boys, on the other hand, often have a
large *circle* of friends. They play sports together and *tend to* do things as a group.
They might feel closer to certain members of the group, but they don't necessarily
seek out one special best friend.

These relationship patterns continue into adulthood. Women *tend to* have a few   3
very close friends. Men don't, however. Instead of spending time with one or two
good friends, men normally get together for group activities. Women take a deep
interest in each other's personal lives. By contrast, men don't usually *disclose*
personal details.

A recent survey supports this argument. When asked to identify their best friend,   4
married women almost always named other women. When *faced* with the same
question, married men named their wives.

Complete the exercises.

A Read these excerpts from the reading. In each excerpt, circle the phrase that signals
contrast. Then draw an arrow between the ideas being contrasted. (*40 points*)

1. . . . little girls usually spend most of their time with one "best friend." Little boys, on

   the other hand, often have a large circle of friends.

2. Women take a deep interest in each other's personal lives. By contrast, men don't

   usually disclose personal details.

B Find the words and phrases in *italics* in the reading. Then complete the sentences.
(*60 points*)

circle (par. 2)	*disclose* (par. 3)	*faced* (par. 4)
numerous (par. 1)	*seek out* (par. 2)	*tend to* (pars. 2, 3)

1. She and her sister don't share friends. They're not in the same social

   _____ .

2. He was _____ with a difficult choice about which college to attend.

3. She doesn't _____ friends, but she is so nice that she always has many
   of them.

4. She asked the man personal questions, but didn't _____ anything
   about herself.

5. He has had _____ interviews but still hasn't found a job.

6. Good friends _____ enjoy the same activities.

Quiz • Unit 6

Name: _____

Date: _____

Read the text.

1   In his writings, Dr. Oliver Sacks – a well-known medical researcher and writer – describes two types of brain *disorders* related to communication. One type of disorder is called "agnosia." People with this disorder cannot attach meaning or emotion to another person's *tone of voice*. The other type of brain disorder, called "aphasia," makes it difficult for people who suffer from it to understand the words spoken by other people.

2   Interestingly, patients who suffer from agnosia often fail to understand the meaning of what people say to them, even though they may understand the words perfectly. On the other hand, aphasiacs may not *comprehend* actual words, but they are usually experts at understanding the *message* that someone is trying to communicate. This is because aphasiacs have an amazing ability to "read" a speaker's *tone of voice*, *gestures*, and facial expressions. In fact, an aphasiac's performance may be so *convincing* that it's hard to tell that he or she suffers from a communicative disorder.

Complete the exercises.

A Mark each statement *T* (true) or *F* (false). (*40 points*)

_____ 1. Agnosia patients have trouble understanding the actual words that people speak.

_____ 2. Aphasiacs find it more difficult to understand spoken words than agnosiacs do.

_____ 3. Patients with agnosia can easily understand the emotion in someone's voice.

_____ 4. People may not notice that the person they are speaking to has aphasia.

B Find the words in *italics* in the reading. Then complete the sentences. (*60 points*)

comprehend (par. 2)   *convincing* (par. 2)   *disorders* (par. 1)
message (par. 2)   *tone of voice* (par. 1 & 2)   *gestures* (par. 3)

1. Please don't use that _____. It makes me think you're angry with me.

2. Today, doctors know how to treat many _____ related to the heart.

3. The same _____ can have different meanings in different cultures.

4. She couldn't _____ what the teacher was saying because he spoke too quickly.

5. I didn't hear everything she said, but her body language communicated her _____ very clearly.

6. The actor who played the father was excellent. His performance was completely _____ .

Quiz • Unit 7

Read the text.

It's *undeniable* that we all lie occasionally, and sometimes our *motives* are not   1
very *admirable*. I learned the hard way. I once got caught lying in order to impress
someone, and it was terribly embarrassing.

I attended a college where skiing was a popular sport, and many students were   2
expert skiers. Unfortunately, I could not *count myself a member* of that group. At
best, I was an intermediate-level skier.

One night, a group of us were sitting around and talking about skiing. I was   3
trying desperately to impress one of the guys. Although my skiing ability was
mediocre, my ability to *exaggerate* was not. Without thinking, I made a ridiculous
claim: I gave him the impression that I was *one step away* from competing in
the Olympics.

A week later, I *bumped into* him on the ski slopes. I will never forget the look on   4
his face as he watched me begin my painful *descent*. He didn't have to say a word.
My *humiliation* was punishment enough.

Complete the exercises.

A Put the events in order. Number the sentences from *1* (first event) to *5* (last event).
(*50 points*)

_____ a. The writer got caught in a lie.

_____ b. The writer told a lie.

_____ c. The writer was talking to some students at her college.

_____ d. The writer wanted another student to like her.

_____ e. The writer was embarrassed and ashamed of herself.

B Find the words and phrases in *italics* in the reading. Then circle the correct meanings.
(*50 points*)

1. When something is *undeniable*, it is **true / unusual**.

2. Your *motive* for doing something is your **reason for / fear of** doing it.

3. When you do something *admirable*, you think it is **right / wrong**.

4. When you *count yourself a member* of a group of people, you feel like you
   belong to / are an extra person in the group.

5. If your ability is *mediocre*, you are **not very talented / very talented**.

6. When you *exaggerate* your skill, you make it seem **better / worse** than it really is.

7. When you are *one step away* from doing something, you **almost / fail to** do it.

8. When you *bump into* someone, you **meet the person by chance /
   almost hit the person**.

9. When you begin your *descent*, you start to go **up / down**.

10. *Humiliation* is a feeling of great **pride / embarrassment**.

Quiz • Unit 8

Name: _____

Date: _____

Read the text.

1   Knowing appropriate table manners is especially important when you travel. What is *courteous* in one culture might be considered rude in another. In order to avoid offending your host or fellow diners, it's important to learn some basic dining etiquette. Here are a few general rules to follow in most situations.

    a. Wait for the others to begin the meal before picking up your eating *utensils*. Once the others have begun, watch how fast they are eating, and try to maintain the same *pace*.

    b. Try a little bit of everything. If you don't like a particular dish, don't take a second *helping*.

    c. Reaching across the table or reaching in front of someone is generally thought of as bad manners. Instead, ask for the item you want to be passed to you.

    d. Keep your eating area as clean as possible. Avoid putting bones or anything from your plate onto the table. If there is something in your mouth that you cannot swallow, such as a bone, *subtly* put it back on your plate or in your napkin and continue eating.

Complete the exercises.

A For each statement, write the letter of the rule in the text that the guest should read. (*50 points*)

_____ 1. When offered a dish, the guest says, "I'm sorry, but I don't like vegetables."

_____ 2. The guest finishes eating 10 minutes before everyone else at the table.

_____ 3. The guest picks out favorite vegetables, and then passes the dish to the next person.

_____ 4. The guest reaches for the salt and pepper, which are at the end of the table.

_____ 5. The guest eats half of a piece of bread and then puts the rest on the table.

B Find the words in *italics* in the reading. Then circle the letters of the correct meanings. (*50 points*)

1. *courteous* (introduction)   a. polite   b. not polite

2. *utensils* (rule a)   a. plates, glasses, or bowls   b. knives, forks, spoons, or chopsticks

3. *pace* (rule a)   a. speed   b. amount of food

4. *helping* (rule b)   a. dish   b. portion of food

5. *subtly* (rule d)   a. without being noticed   b. openly

Quiz • Unit 9

Read the text.

When I was a child, I loved to get scared. It's a good thing I enjoyed it, because   1
my family had a *hair-raising* tradition of frightening each other. Halloween was an
especially exciting time of year. My father would dress up in a *gruesome* costume
and visit all the children's parties, where he was known as "Mr. Halloween." When
the children finally finished screaming, they always *begged* him to come back and
terrorize them again.

One year, though, he went too far. For some reason, we had a very real-looking,   2
life-sized doll's head down in the basement of our house. My father attached
the head to the end of a long *pole*. Then he stood under our neighbor's window,
holding up the pole so that the head appeared to float in front of the glass. When
our neighbor looked out and saw the head, she was nearly scared to death. She
screamed, her face turned white, and she couldn't speak for some time. After that
experience, "Mr. Halloween" took an early *retirement*.

Complete the exercises.

A Check (✓) the statements that you can infer are true based on information in the
reading. (*40 points*)

_____ 1. The children enjoyed being scared by the writer's father.

_____ 2. The writer loved dolls.

_____ 3. The neighbor did not expect to see anything scary outside her window.

_____ 4. As an adult, the writer does not like Halloween.

B Find the words in *italics* in the reading. Then complete the sentences. (*60 points*)

hair-raising (par. 1)   *gruesome* (par. 1)   *begged* (par. 1)
terrorize (par. 1)   *pole* (par. 2)   *retirement* (par. 2)

1. Children, please don't _____ your little brother with your scary stories.

2. I don't like the _____ scenes of bloody fighting in war movies.

3. He loves _____ because now he can spend time with his grandchildren
   instead of going to work.

4. He told a _____ story about the night he heard noises in the attic.

5. The flag was raised to the top of the _____.

6. The children _____ me so much that I finally let them have
   more candy.

Quiz • Unit 10

Name: _____

Date: _____

Read the text.

1   Do you believe in the paranormal, or are you a skeptic? In the dictionary, *skeptic* means "a person who doubts the truth or value of an idea or belief." Some people are skeptics about the paranormal. In fact, there is a society called The Skeptics Society, which is an organization of leading scientists, scholars, and other professionals who question the existence of the paranormal. For example, they don't believe in psychics or near-death experiences. Writers for their publication, *Skeptic Magazine*, explore "extraordinary claims and revolutionary ideas." Contributors to the magazine also write about meditation and other uncommon states of mind. The goal of the society is to show how science can explain "paranormal" events and experiences.

2   The editors describe their magazine as an educational tool. Their goal is to teach the public to be able to tell the difference between true science and what they consider to be "junk science." Many of the articles provide scientific explanations for things that appear to be supernatural, such as telekinesis and visions.

Complete the exercises.

A Mark each statement *T* (true) or *F* (false). *(40 points)*

_____ 1. Many writers for *Skeptic Magazine* believe in ghosts.

_____ 2. Many scientists and scholars read the magazine.

_____ 3. Writers for the magazine are skeptical about the supernatural.

_____ 4. Articles in the magazine teach people how to become psychics.

B Find the words in the reading that are similar to the words in *italics*. *(30 points)*

1. *doubt v.* (par. 1)   _____ *v.* (par. 1)

2. *contributors n.* (par. 1)   _____ *n.* (par. 1)

3. *publication n.* (par. 1)   _____ *n.* (par. 1 & par. 2)

C Match each word or phrase with an example of it from the box. *(30 points)*

a. telekinesis	b. meditation	c. researchers

_____ 1. scholars

_____ 2. state of mind

_____ 3. the supernatural

Quiz • Unit 11

Read the text.

There is a debate in many parts of the English-speaking world about the best   1
way to educate the children of non-English speaking immigrants.

On one side of the argument are people who support bilingual education, where   2
children study subjects in their own language. As their English improves, they begin
to study in English and their native tongue. The idea is that this is the most effective
way for students to learn and be successful when they enter *mainstream* classes.

People on the other side of the argument *advocate* English *immersion*. These   3
programs place non-English speaking children in classes where only English is
spoken. The idea is that when students are totally surrounded by a language, they
will learn it more quickly. In most immersion programs, children receive one year
of English instruction in addition to their academic classes.

Experts on each side of the debate continue to claim that their method is   4
superior. As a result, the topic remains controversial.

Complete the exercises.

A Find the words in *italics* in the text. Then circle the correct meanings. (*40 points*)

1. When students learning English enter a *mainstream* class, they study
   in their native tongue / in English / with only non-English speakers.

2. In an English *immersion* program, students are in classes with children and teachers
   who **speak their native language / speak English / are bilingual**.

3. If you *advocate* something, you **want / don't want** it to happen.

4. If you believe one thing is *superior*, you believe it is **better than / equal to /**
   different from another thing.

B What do these words refer to? Write the correct word. (*30 points*)

1. *their* (par. 2, line 2)   _____

2. *they* (par. 2, line 4)   _____

3. *their* (par. 3, line 5)   _____

C Compare the meaning of each pair of sentences. Write *S* (same) or *D* (different).
(*30 points*)

_____ 1. They begin to study in English and their native tongue.
         They learn English before they learn academic material.

_____ 2. When students are surrounded by a language, they learn it more quickly than
         students in bilingual programs.
         Students in immersion programs learn a language faster than students in
         bilingual programs.

_____ 3. Experts on each side of the debate continue to claim that their method is a
         superior way of teaching.
         Education specialists are in agreement about the best way to teach.

Name: _____

Date: _____

Quiz • Unit 12

Read the text.

1   Scientists believe that a dog's sense of smell is far greater than a human's. At Florida State University, researchers are conducting experiments to find out how *acute* a dog's sense of smell really is. They are finding that dogs can *detect* odors at extraordinarily low levels.

2   This discovery could be good news for people with cancer, since cancer cells *emit* a scent that healthy cells do not. Therefore, if dogs can be trained to smell cancer cells, they might be able to alert doctors to the presence of cancer.

3   Scientists started to experiment with training dogs to sniff out cancer when they became aware of situations in which dogs showed an unusual interest in cancerous parts of their owners' bodies. Their experiments are showing some encouraging results. At a laboratory in California, one dog trained to detect lung cancer by smelling a patient's breath has had an 85 percent success rate.

Complete the exercises.

A Find the words in *italics* in the text. Then complete the sentences. *(30 points)*

acute (par. 1)   *emit* (par. 2)   *detect* (par. 1)

1. The alarm will _____ a loud sound if anyone tries to break in.

2. The photograph was old and faded, but I could still _____ the image.

3. Her _____ eyesight helped her read the small print on the board.

B What do these words refer to? Write the correct words. *(30 points)*

1. *They* (par. 1, line 3)   _____

2. *they* (par. 2, line 3)   _____

3. *Their* (par. 3, line 3)   _____

C Check (✓) the statements that you can infer are true based on information in the reading. *(20 points)*

_____ 1. Dogs can smell things that humans cannot smell.

_____ 2. All dogs can be trained to smell cancerous cells.

_____ 3. Researchers will continue to experiment with dogs and their sense of smell.

D Check (✓) the writer's main purpose in the reading. *(20 points)*

_____ 1. to explain the details of some medical research with dogs

_____ 2. to show that dogs may be able to be trained to smell cancer

_____ 3. to encourage cancer patients to have dogs

Unit Quiz Answers

Unit 1 Quiz

A

2

B

1. T   2. F   3. T   4. F   5. T

C

1. happy and energetic
2. call out names
3. told
4. look good
5. embarrassed
6. improve

Unit 2 Quiz

A

1. are not sure
2. good
3. doing it yourself
4. wants to become a teacher
5. have to

B

3

C

1. F   2. T   3. F   4. F

Unit 3 Quiz

A

1, 2, 5, 6

B

1. f   2. d   3. a   4. b   5. e   6. c

Unit 4 Quiz

A

1. T   2. P   3. T   4. T

B

1. b   2. b   3. a   4. b   5. c   6. a

Unit 5 Quiz

A

1. [. . . little girls usually spend most of their time with one "best friend."] [Little boys, (on the other hand,) often have a large circle of friends.]

2. [Women take a deep interest in each other's personal lives.] (By contrast,) [men don't usually disclose details.]

B

1. circle
2. faced
3. seek out
4. disclose
5. numerous
6. tend to

Unit 6 Quiz

A

1. F   2. T   3. F   4. T

B

1. tone of voice
2. disorders
3. gestures
4. comprehend
5. message
6. convincing

Unit 7 Quiz

A

a. 4   b. 3   c. 1   d. 2   e. 5

B

1. true
2. reason for
3. right
4. belong to
5. not very talented
6. better
7. almost
8. meet the person by chance
9. down
10. embarrassment

Unit 8 Quiz

A

1. b   2. a   3. b   4. c   5. d

B

1. a   2. b   3. a   4. b   5. a

Unit 9 Quiz

A

1, 3

B

1. terrorize
2. gruesome
3. retirement
4. hair-raising
5. pole
6. begged

Unit 10 Quiz

A

1. F   2. T   3. T   4. F

B

1. question
2. writers
3. magazine

C

1. c   2. b   3. a

Unit 11 Quiz

A

1. in English
2. speak English
3. want
4. better than

B

1. children
2. students
3. children

C

1. D   2. S   3. D

Unit 12 Quiz

A

1. emit
2. detect
3. acute

B

1. researchers
2. dogs
3. Scientists

C

1, 3

D

2

www.ingramcontent.com/pod-product-compliance
Ingram Content Group UK Ltd.
Pitfield, Milton Keynes, MK11 3LW, UK
UKHW052101280225
455719UK00014B/456